A Year of Flowers™

4 Letter to Readers **5** Author Bio **6** Getting Started **8** Tips, Tricks & Time-Savers

January
Masking

11 Thank You Bouquet

13 Treasured Roses

15 Happy Birthday!

February
Flower Lattice

16 Beautiful Valentine

18 Sunflower Hello

19 Just for Being You

March
Direct-to-Stamp

20 Get Well Soon

22 Happy Day

23 Daisies for Baby

April
Sponged Scenes

24 Here Comes the Sun

26 Easter Glory

27 Make a Wish

May
Paper Tole

28 Paper Roses

30 Crazy Daisies

31 Your Special Day

June
Faux Finishes

32 You're a Blessing Dad

34 For You

35 Blessings

July
Embossing

36 Celebrate

38 Gilded Lilies

39 Welcome Little One

August
Reverse Masking

40 Floral Fantasy

42 Beautiful Friend

43 Congrats!

September
Easel Cards

44 For You

46 Beautiful Day

47 Pop-Art Birthday

October
Crayon Resist

48 Irresistible Daisies

50 Sunset Spectrum

51 Moonlit Flowers

November
Bleach Stamping

52 Grateful

54 Sunflowers in Autumn

55 Bleached Roses

December
Vellum

56 Frosted Poinsettias

58 Stained Glass Elegance

59 Celebrate the Beauty

60 Dates to Remember

64 Buyer's Guide

Letter to Readers

I fell in love with card making in the spring of 2003 at a stamping workshop. Little did I know then that this passion for stamping would develop over the years into opportunities to eventually illustrate my own stamps for Gina K. Designs and share my vision for them with people around the world on my blog, and now, through this book! My favorite stamp set that I've created by far is A Year of Flowers, which is used in every sample in the pages that follow. With this one timeless floral set that lends itself to a multitude of techniques, you'll be able to design cards for every season and occasion. It was a joy to create this year of cards with you in mind, organized by month and holiday, and showcasing techniques that build on each other throughout the year. This book brings a variety of colors, styles and levels of difficulty that I hope will appeal to all crafters, regardless of how new or seasoned you may be.

Choosing a store-bought card will never bring the satisfaction that making a card does, nor will it have the meaning for your recipient as something you poured a little bit of yourself into. Beyond a few basic design principles, there really are no rules about what to do or when to use certain colors; the art just needs to reflect what makes you (and the person you are creating it for) unique! Personal touches that make YOU happy are what will make your designs shine.

Additionally, you'll never forget a birthday or anniversary again with the built-in Dates to Remember pages I've included in the back. You'll have all your important dates at your fingertips, with layouts, ideas and step-by-step instructions for cards right in front of you! You can bet I'll be using this throughout the year to remind myself not only of days to remember, but of tried-and-true techniques that enable me to jump-start a design with a particular layout or color combination. This will help when I need a card (but might not be feeling so creative), as well as inspire me to tweak an existing design to make something entirely new.

My prayer is that the projects in this book will make you feel more confident and excited about creating your own cards, whether it's following a tutorial to make an exact copy of a design, making significant changes, or just browsing for ideas. I encourage you to take a design you like and adapt it to any other occasion or season you see fit. The flower images are so flexible, for example, that you can substitute the rose and pink in a May design with a sunflower and autumnal color scheme to create a beautiful Thanksgiving card. Peeking ahead *is* encouraged! I'm excited to see where this book takes you! I invite you to visit my blog, melaniemuenchinger.blogspot.com and email me photos of your own creations, and I hope you will share them online to inspire others. The joy of crafting and stamping is all about passing it on.

Hugs and blessings,

Melanie

Celebrate the *beauty* of the season.

Author Bio
Melanie Muenchinger

PHOTO COPYRIGHT © MARTY EISENBERGER

I began stamping in 2003, but have had a lifelong love affair with paper crafting and flowers! In 2008, I started working as a senior designer and illustrator for Gina K. Designs. Upon publication of this book, I've created almost 50 stamp sets exclusively for Gina K. Designs. With sets ranging from clean graphic to realistic nature images, whimsical animals and decorative elements, I am always working to put a fresh spin on a theme or to start a trend. A Year of Flowers is one of Gina K.'s best-selling stamp sets, and it has been featured on PBS and in various crafting publications by numerous designers. My design work can often be found in the pages of *CardMaker* and *Crafts n' Things*. You can check out more of my past work and ongoing projects, tutorials and inspiration for all my stamps and other fabulous Gina K. Designs sets on my blog, Hands, Head and Heart, at www.melaniemuenchinger.blogspot.com. I live in Austin, Texas, with my husband and two sons, and I'm grateful to be a stay-at-home mom who gets to draw and play with stamps and paper for a living. Many thanks to all our Gina K. and StampTV fans and customers who add new life and inspiration to these floral images every day through their stamping, and to those who made me believe this set could be a whole book! Thanks to friends and family too numerous to mention who have supported this project, given advice, offered encouragement and lifted up prayers for me all along the way. Thank you God for your unfailing love, abundant gifts and gorgeous flowers!

Getting Started

If you are new to card making, a very rich and rewarding adventure awaits you! Locating a few basic supplies and a place to sit and work are all you need to begin enjoying this craft. Almost all products used in this book are available online at Gina K. Designs. General supplies like adhesive, cutting tools and paper can also be found at any local craft store.

A Year of Flowers is a precut rubber stamp set, deeply etched and mounted on cling vinyl, ready to be used with acrylic blocks. Flowers are appropriate for any occasion you might need to send a card, and the variety of floral images for every season that are included in this book make it one you will keep on your desk year-round! Recommended block sizes for this set are 2½ inches and 3½ inches with the smallest images fitting on the 2½-inch blocks, and largest flowers fitting on the 3½-inch blocks. These sizes are also suitable for most other cling images and greetings. I prefer round, grid-lined, finger-grip blocks, but square blocks work well also. You may use just one large block for all images, but many find it easier to use a smaller block for small stamps to prevent rocking and overstamping.

You will also need:
- Black or brown ink pad
- Coloring medium of choice: markers, colored pencils, watercolors
- Smooth cardstock in desired colors
- Paper cutter
- Scissors
- Paper adhesive
- Adhesive foam dots
- Scratch paper
- Masking material or sticky notes

Additional embellishments & fun extras:
- Ribbon
- Buttons
- Printed papers
- Sponges
- Colored ink pads
- Glossy cardstock
- Punches
- Dies

The use of printed paper is minimal in these samples because certain patterns are not always available or often retire, but also because, as a stamper at heart, my instinct most often is to create my own patterns with stamps. Nothing will be quite as coordinated as a pattern made with the stamps you use in your focal point! Additionally, I wanted these designs to be easy for you to recreate exactly as you see them, without a lot of shopping around. I encourage you to use your stamps to make your own backgrounds, as well as incorporating the various techniques for different looks. If you love printed papers, by all means mix colors, patterns and styles you like with these images, as everything looks great with flowers! The same goes for embellishments and ribbon. I've chosen ones that are most commonly available anywhere, and never go out of style, like pearls, rhinestones and gingham. An added bonus is that they are also all very affordable!

Prepping a Precut Rubber Stamp Set

Pop individual stamps out of stamp sheet and remove paper backing from each piece in the set. Place all images onto the plastic binder sheet included. You may want to store this in a binder or binder box along with the image sheet. Stamp each of your images onto scratch paper and cut them out. These will work as masks which we cover in the January set of projects. Save them in a locking plastic bag with your stamps to reuse again and again.

Optional

There are several more sets from Gina K. Designs that coordinate with A Year of Flowers to expand your paper-crafting possibilities and creativity.

Say It With Flowers: sentiments and verses for every occasion.

Arranged With Love: ornate flower-filled frame with elegant sentiments to match.

Pressed Flowers: bold images that match A Year of Flowers' images; great for various technique and two-step stamping with the A Year of Flowers set.

Festive Frame: wintery flower frame with holiday sentiments and an opening for framing photos, greetings and stamped images.

A Beautiful Life: tulip frame with spring and year-round sentiments.

Buds and Vases: three containers for arrangements and new flowers.

Spring Basket: a basket for arrangements plus bunches and smaller individual elements that match the spring blooms in A Year of Flowers.

All stamped sentiments used in the following samples are available through Gina K. Designs, the majority coming from the sets I mentioned above as well as a few others. Feel free to substitute your own writing, rub-ons, stickers, other stamps or to print your own text. A Year of Flowers contains the greetings "with love" and "for you" which will fit any occasion.

The layouts and techniques in this book can also be used for designing cards with other stamps. While I believe A Year of Flowers is one of the most versatile sets for creating stamped cards on the market, you can get started applying the techniques right away with other images in your collection. The techniques I've chosen are the ones I love, and after eight years of experience, use most often. They are musts for any stamper. They are easy, quick and produce stunning results. *

Tips, Tricks & Time-Savers

Time-Savers & Quick Fixes

Don't start over, boo-boos are part of the territory of "handmade!" After eight years, I still from time to time get a smudge on my card from inky fingers or get a less than perfect stamped image, but these experiences have given me a lot of practice turning these mistakes around! Often the "fix" allows for a new and unexpected turn in your design that thankfully is even better than what you planned, so roll with it, baby!

Smudge on Your Mat

This is the most common offender when you're playing with ink! If it's near the edge, just crop a little closer to cut off the mark! A smudge can be frustrating when you were hoping to make a single-layer card, but trimming the mat just a bit smaller and layering the trimmed piece onto a card base that picks up one of the colors in your focal point is always a safe bet. If it's too close to your focal point to do that, try covering it with a stamped tag with a sentiment. Whether it is die-cut, punched or simply trimmed in a square by hand, popped up on foam dots over the smudge, this added layer is always lovely.

You can also add a large embellishment like a button, or you can wrap a length of ribbon around it or add a bow.

If it's right next to or on the image itself, and a tag is not an option, stamp some extra leaves or flowers, and place them over the mark. This extra dimension really brings your bouquet to life.

Fixing Uneven or Incomplete Stamped Images

Keep fine-tip pens or markers handy in the same color inks as your pads to fill in a small detail or make a connection; it's often just a small line or two. If the missing part of the image is definitely beyond your

Folding & Mat Size

A2 Size: 4¼ x 5½ inches

This is the most common card size for stampers and paper crafters, most likely because one sheet of 8½ x 11 inches yields exactly two card bases when cut in half! These cards require little postage to mail, have plenty of room to write in, and are not too intimidating a space to add designs to if you are a beginner!

Top-Fold Card: 4¼ x 11 inches, scored at 5½ inches
Side-Fold Card: 8½ inches, scored at 4¼ inches, x 5½ inches

I choose how thick my border will be based on how delicate or bold the lines in the stamped image and sentiment are—chunky stamps can handle "chunkier" mats, but for fine lines, I like a small reveal. For instance, when using a greeting with a font that is only ⅟₁₆ inch wide, stamped in black, adding a ⅟₁₆-inch black mat underneath looks really sharp! I also factor in how prominent I want that particular color mat to be in my design. Sometimes I change my mind as I work on the card in order to balance my colors and layout, but I always start bigger and then trim down if needed, since you can't go back! I don't love to measure, but getting familiar with a few dimensions will have you cropping with confidence.

Layering Mats for A2: 4⅛ x 5⅜ inches, 4 x 5¼ inches, 3¾ x 5 inches
Square Card: 4¼ x 8½ inches scored at 4¼ inches, one sheet will yield two cards
Square Mats: 4 x 4 inches, 3¾ x 3¾ inches, 3½ x 3½ inches, 3¼ x 3¼ inches

drawing or editing abilities, and you don't want to redo it, try stamping the image again and popping it up over the first. The added dimension really makes your card special.

However, if you haven't gotten far, and the fix is not convenient or obvious, just remember that all paper has two sides, so if you really can't fix it, flip it over and start anew!

How Do I Find the Time to Make Cards?

As a mom of two boys, I know "busy!" But everyone benefits from having some sort of creative outlet, and there are lots of ways to knock out handmade cards, even if it's just for a few minutes at a time, creating parts piecemeal and assembling them later. It's wonderful to have some die cuts or colored images ready when you have a chance to sit down and craft! Cutting out paper flowers while listening to a little music at the end of the day is very meditative and relaxing; you don't really have to think about it, but you are getting something done, which is always a bonus. How about stamping some sentiment tags while watching a program with your family, or bringing a few stamped images and some markers outside while you watch the kids play? Involve children who love to be helpers and would be eager to get inky and learn the techniques in these chapters! Paper crafting is a wonderful way to bond, and card making reinforces keeping in touch with loved ones in a personal way. Plan a girls' night and turn the stamping into a party. The list of ways to incorporate this into your life just gets longer as you go deeper into the craft and develop your art and style.

Another problem you might run into is that when you do have time you might not have any mojo! Even simple things like cutting and scoring a few card bases or addressing your envelopes will make things so much easier when you do decide it's time to sit down and play. That's where this book comes in. Copy cards exactly. You'll find the more cards you make, the easier it gets, and the more easily the inspiration and ideas flow.

Be sure to really take advantage of the perpetual calendar in the back! Add all your birthdays, anniversaries and dates you know and see how many you'll need per month. It's wonderful to make cards "just because" when the mood strikes, but it is always a great feeling to get ahead! Making a card should be fun, not stressful.

Coloring

Flowers lend themselves to so many terrific techniques and an unlimited number of colors and color combinations. Fortunately, you don't need to be an expert at coloring to achieve great results with these stamps. Whether your favorite medium is Copics® markers, pencils, watercolors or pastels, you will love coloring these images! Although, many people who use this set have told me these flowers practically color themselves because the lines in the image show you exactly where to trace or add colors and shadows. Stamping them on colored paper also produces wonderfully vibrant, colored petals! Throughout the book you will see different ways to color them, with bleach or sponged ink, just to name a few. Left uncolored they make gorgeous patterns and backgrounds.

Color Meanings

Color creates a mood, and you can look to real flowers for inspiration in your yard or photos in books or online. You might even choose a favorite fabric, pattern, work of art or even a fabulous sunset as a color palette to get you started. The majority of the cards in this book use palettes of 2–4 colors to give you lots of ideas for different combinations, but monochromatic cards (one color plus a neutral, like white, or several shades of one color) are always lovely and very easy to make without having to choose other colors and worry about clashing! Beyond colors you associate with popular holidays, here are what certain colors often convey or what moods they produce. I hope this is helpful if you are stuck in a rut or want to really make an impact with color!

Red	Love, enthusiasm, romance
Orange	Energy, warmth
Yellow	Happiness, optimism, encouragement
Green	Relaxation, peace, nature
Blue	Sky, water, cool, dependable
Purple	Uplifting, calming, mystical, regal
Pink	Femininity, youth, joy
Black	Drama, sophistication
White	Purity, clarity, new beginnings
Brown	Wholesome, earthy

tip

Trace around stamped images with pale gray or lavender marker as desired to create a subtle shadow and a wonderful dimensional effect.

January
Thank You Bouquet

Layering stamped images using the masking technique allows you to add depth to your projects. Start by stamping the flowers that are intended to be the focus of your project, followed by stems, leaves and additional blossoms to build a pleasing arrangement.

Materials

Cardstock: yellow, purple, green, white smooth
Masking material
Stamp sets: A Year of Flowers, Arranged With Love
Ink pads: black dye, watermark
Copic® markers: BV02, BV31, G99, RV000, RV29, V17, Y08, Y11, YG03, YR16
Adhesive foam dots
Paper adhesive

tip

Make masks of every image in your stamp set and keep them in a resealable plastic bag with the set so you have them ready for future projects. To quickly create multiple masks for one image, stamp image onto a stack of three sticky notes then trim image, cutting through all three sheets at once.

Form a 4¼ x 5½-inch card from yellow cardstock.

Cut a 4 x 5¼-inch piece from purple cardstock. Using watermark ink, stamp tulips and stems onto purple panel as desired (Photo 1).

Photo 1

Adhere the stamped panel to card front as shown. Using black ink, stamp the following onto masking material: two lilies, three tulips and five stems. Cut out all stamped images from masking material.

Cut a 3 x 3¾-inch piece from white smooth cardstock. Stamp two lilies onto white panel as shown (Photo 2).

Photo 2

Cover both lilies with masking-material lilies.

In the same manner, stamp three tulips onto white panel, overlapping masked lilies as shown (Photo 3).

Photo 3

Cover tulips on panel with masking tulips (Photo 4).

Photo 4

In the same manner, stamp stems onto panel as shown. Cover stems with masking stems and stamp leaves onto panel. Remove all masks. Color images using markers (Photos 5–7).

Photo 5

Photo 6

Photo 7

tip

When creating arrangements, think in odd numbers: one, three and five, which are more pleasing to the eye than even numbers, which tend to look more static.

tip

Complicated arrangements are not necessary for a beautiful card. A single flower can capture your attention and is perfect for a quick "need it now!" card with a sentiment. If using more than one flower, they should be placed at different heights to draw your eye around the card. There are, of course, exceptions to this, a good one being when you send a card to a couple; two flowers have beautiful symbolism for an anniversary or wedding! Be sure to stamp them at different heights and to tilt them at slightly different angles, especially if using the same image, so they don't look exactly alike.

Adhere panel to purple cardstock; trim a small border. Adhere to yellow cardstock; trim a border. Attach to card front with foam dots.

Using black ink, stamp "Thanks" onto green cardstock. Cut out word and adhere to card front as shown. ✳

Sources: Cardstock and stamp sets from Gina K. Designs; Memento dye ink pad and VersaMark watermark ink pad from Tsukineko LLC; markers from Imagination International Inc.; foam dots and paper adhesive from Tombow USA.

Treasured Roses

Sympathy cards are not our favorite projects to make. Unfortunately, these events are part of life and often unexpected. To be prepared for a time when you may not feel like making a card, create a few using beautiful images, colors and sentiments that will convey what's in your heart.

Materials
Cardstock: light blue, white, dark brown
Masking material
Stamp sets: A Year of Flowers,
     A Beautiful Life
Dye ink pads: dark brown, tan distress,
     blue distress
Copic® marker: W-3
Die templates: Petite Scalloped Ovals LG
     (#S4-139), Petite Ovals LG (#S4-138)
Die-cutting and embossing machine
Craft sponge
Adhesive foam dots
Paper adhesive

When
someone
you love
becomes a
memory,
the memory
becomes a
treasure.

Form a 4¼ x 5½-inch card from light blue cardstock.

Cut a 4 x 5⅛-inch piece from white cardstock. Using tan ink, stamp roses randomly onto white panel; allow some roses to run off edges of panel. Clean stamp. In the same manner and using blue ink, stamp two roses onto white panel (Photo 1).

Photo 1

Sponge tan ink around edges and lightly across entire white panel (Photo 2).

Photo 2

Using desired color of ink, stamp a rose onto masking material; cut out. Place rose mask over a rose on white panel. Using corresponding color of ink, stamp leaves onto masked rose, over-lapping mask. Repeat until all roses have leaves (Photo 3).

Photo 3

Adhere white panel to dark brown cardstock; trim a small border. Adhere to card front.

Using 2¼ x 3¼-inch Petite Scalloped Ovals LG die template, die-cut and emboss a scalloped oval from dark brown cardstock.

Stamp sentiment onto white cardstock with dark brown ink. Using desired Petite Ovals LG die template, die-cut and emboss an oval around sentiment making sure oval will fit onto dark brown

scalloped oval. Attach ovals together using foam dots. Adhere to card front as shown.

Stamp two roses onto light blue cardstock with dark brown ink; in the same manner, stamp four leaves onto white cardstock. Cut out roses and leaves. Color shadows on all stamped images using marker. Layer and attach to card front as shown using foam dots. ✳

Sources: Cardstock and stamp sets from Gina K. Designs; distress ink pads from Ranger Industries Inc.; marker from Imagination International Inc.; die templates from Spellbinders™ Paper Arts; adhesive foam dots from Plaid Enterprises Inc.; paper adhesive from Tombow USA.

Happy Birthday!

Don't be afraid to stamp your focal points on pastel papers instead of white for a striking effect. Colored cardstock picks up coloring very nicely, intensifies it evenly and saves you time in not having to fill in a base color for your image.

tip

Adhesive dots are my go-to craft supply and one that fits every budget! These inexpensive bits of dimensional foam work double time as adhesive as well as taking your project to another level—literally! I almost never make a card without at least one raised element, whether it's a mat with my stamped focal point, just part of an image or the sentiment. In my opinion, they are more versatile and have more value than any ribbon or embellishment. That tiny lift takes your card from flat to fabulous!

Sources: Cardstock, A Year of Flowers stamp set and Arranged With Love stamp set from Gina K. Designs; Memento brown dye ink pad from Tsukineko LLC; Copic® markers from Imagination International Inc.; self-adhesive pearls and adhesive foam dots from Mark Richards Enterprises Inc.; Classic Squares LG die templates (#S4-126) from Spellbinders™ Paper Arts; double-sided adhesive from Tombow USA.

February
Beautiful Valentine

Create a bouquet with this lattice technique to give your handcrafted greeting card extra detail and dimension.

Materials
Cardstock: black, white, red, green
Masking material
Stamp sets: A Year of Flowers,
    A Beautiful Life
Black dye ink pad
Copic® marker: C-3
Silver self-adhesive rhinestone
Labels Fourteen die templates (#S4-290)
Die-cutting and embossing machine
Scoring tool
Adhesive foam dots
Paper adhesive

you make life *beautiful*

Form a 4¼ x 5½-inch card from black cardstock. Cut a 4 x 5¼-inch piece of white cardstock; set aside.

Cut a 4 x 5-inch piece from red cardstock. Stamp five roses onto red panel, reinking and rotating image each time (Photo 1). *Note: Stamped roses should just barely touch each other.* Stamp one or two roses onto masking material; cut out.

Photo 1

Cover roses on red panel with masking roses. Stamp roses on either side of each masked rose, overlapping masked roses and extending past edges of red panel, creating rose clusters. Remove mask (Photo 2).

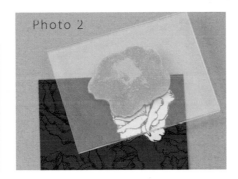

Photo 2

Use marker to create additional shading on roses as desired.

Cut around rose clusters, keeping overlapping roses together and snipping in between roses just touching (Photo 3).

Photo 3

Lay rose clusters onto 4 x 5¼-inch white cardstock panel; referring to photo, trim edges as needed. Using paper adhesive, adhere a cluster of roses to upper right corner of white panel, only applying adhesive to center of roses. Attach remaining rose clusters to white panel as shown using foam dots (Photo 4).

Photo 4

Stamp seven leaves onto green cardstock and cut out. Apply paper adhesive to ends of leaves and adhere to card front as shown, tucking leaves under rose clusters (Photo 5).

Photo 5

Stamp sentiment onto white cardstock. Using 1¾ x 2¾-inch Labels Fourteen die template, die-cut a label around sentiment. With long edge of label horizontal on work surface, score a vertical line ¼ inch from left edge. Mountain-fold at scored line. Attach sentiment label to white panel as shown with foam dots; wrap and secure folded section of label to back of panel using paper adhesive. Embellish sentiment with rhinestone. Adhere assembled panel to card front with paper adhesive. ✳

Sources: Cardstock and stamp sets from Gina K. Designs; Memento dye ink pad from Tsukineko LLC; marker from Imagination International Inc.; self-adhesive rhinestone from Mark Richards Enterprises Inc.; die templates from Spellbinders™ Paper Arts; paper adhesive from Tombow USA.

Sunflower Hello

Give your lattice flower design a twist by incorporating the spotlight technique and punched shapes to add color and dimension.

Form a 5½ x 4¼-inch card from kraft cardstock.

Cut a 5¼ x 4-inch piece from yellow cardstock. Starting in the middle, stamp sunflowers onto yellow panel (Photo 1). ***Note:*** *Allow sunflowers to slightly overlap and extend off edges of panel as shown.*

Photo 1

Trim around sunflowers on yellow panel, leaving them attached where they overlap (Photo 2).

Photo 2

Attach to card front using foam dots. ***Note:*** *It is OK if some of the sunflowers get cut apart as the lattice*

will piece back together when it is adhered to card front.

Stamp four sunflowers onto rust cardstock. Using a 1-inch circle punch, punch center from each sunflower (Photo 3).

Photo 3

Materials
Cardstock: kraft, yellow, green, rust, dark brown, blue
Stamp sets: A Year of Flowers, A Beautiful Life
Dark brown dye ink pad
Circle punches: 1-inch, 1¼-inch, 1⅜-inch
Adhesive foam dots
Paper adhesive

*tip

Spotlighting is bringing focus to just part of an image using color, a shaped die or a punch.

Stamp five sunflowers onto green cardstock. Using a 1¼-inch circle punch, punch center from each sunflower (Photo 4).

Photo 4

Using foam dots, attach punched centers of sunflowers to card front as shown; trim as needed to align edges.

Stamp "hello" onto blue cardstock. Punch a 1¼ inch circle around word. Punch a 1⅜-inch circle from dark brown cardstock. Adhere circles together; using two stacked foam dots, adhere to lower right corner of card. ✳

Sources: Cardstock and stamp sets from Gina K. Designs; adhesive foam dots from Plaid Enterprises Inc.

tip

Using adhesives foam dots to attach spotlighting elements adds interesting depth to a card.

Just for Being You

Cut out a stamped and masked vine of flowers to create a pretty border. Accent the flower centers with glitter for extra sparkle.

Sources: Cardstock, A Year of Flowers stamp set and Arranged With Love stamp set from Gina K. Designs; Memento dye ink pad from Tsukineko LLC; Copic® markers from Imagination International Inc.; white pen and glitter glue from Ranger Industries Inc.; self-adhesive pearls from Mark Richards Enterprises Inc.; Standard Circles LG die templates (#S4-114) from Spellbinders™ Paper Arts; adhesive foam dots from Plaid Enterprises Inc; double-sided adhesive from Tombow USA.

March
Get Well Soon

Coloring images direct-to-stamp with water-based markers allows placement of color exactly where you want and creates a soft watercolor look when spritzed with water before stamping.

get well soon

Materials
Cardstock: lavender, purple, white
Stamp sets: A Year of Flowers, Say It
    With Flowers
Dye ink markers: light blue, lavender,
    purple, green
5 (2mm) silver nailheads
Die templates: Lacey Squares (#S4-295),
    Fancy Tags (#S4 235)
Die-cutting and embossing machine
Spray bottle filled with water
Watercolor brush
Scoring board with scoring tool
Adhesive foam dots
Paper adhesive

Form a 4¼ x 4¼-inch card from lavender cardstock.

Using 4¼ x 4¼-inch Lacey Squares die template, die-cut a square from purple cardstock. Adhere to card front.

Cut a 3⅝ x 3⅝-inch piece from white cardstock. Use light blue marker to color top section of flower stamp (Photo 1).

Photo 1

Color middle section of flower lavender and bottom section purple (Photo 2).

Photo 2

Spritz flower image lightly with water and stamp a flower onto white panel as shown. Repeat to stamp second flower (Photo 3).

Photo 3

Color stem green and spritz with water. Stamp stem onto white panel. Repeat to stamp a second stem and two leaves. Dampen watercolor brush and gently blend color on stems and leaves (Photo 4).

Photo 4

If desired, add more color by running a wet watercolor brush across the tip of a green marker and applying color to stems and leaves (Photo 5).

Photo 5

Using scoreboard and scoring tool, score a border ⅛ inch from edges of white panel. Adhere to card front.

Color sentiment stamp with purple marker; stamp sentiment onto white cardstock. Using ⅞ x 3½-inch Fancy Tags die template, die-cut and emboss a tag around sentiment. Attach to card front as shown using foam dots.

Embellish card with nailheads. ✳

Sources: Cardstock and stamp sets from Gina K. Designs; Memento dye ink markers from Tsukineko LLC; nailheads from Mark Richards Enterprises Inc.; Mini Mister spray bottle from Ranger Industries Inc.; die templates from Spellbinders™ Paper Arts; scoring board with scoring tool from Scor-Pal Products; paper adhesive from Tombow USA.

tip

If desired, spray additional water onto colored stamp before stamping to create a more watercolored effect.

Happy Day

Turn a daisy into a completely new flower with this simple, direct-to-stamp technique which allows for precision inking and more versatility with your images.

*tip

The sweet ladybugs in this set can be added anywhere you need a little pop of color! Crawling on a petal or along a border, they will bring your card to life!

have a

happy

day

Materials
Cardstock: yellow, red, black, white, kraft
Masking material
Stamp sets: A Year of Flowers, Say It With Flowers, A Beautiful Life
Black dye ink marker
Copic® markers: E57, G94, R29, Y08, Y17, YG23
Large red button
21 inches ⅝-inch-wide white/black gingham ribbon
Adhesive foam dots
Paper adhesive

Form a 4¼ x 5½-inch card from yellow cardstock.

Cut a 2⅜ x 4½-inch piece from red cardstock and a 2½ x 4¼-inch piece from black cardstock. Adhere cardstock pieces to card front as shown.

Cut a 3¾ x 4½-inch piece from white cardstock. Using black dye ink marker, color desired portion of flower stamp (Photo 1).

Photo 1

Huff on stamp and stamp image onto white panel as shown. In the same manner and referring to photo, stamp a second flower onto white panel and two flowers onto masking material.

Mask flowers on image panel. Color stem stamp with black marker in the same manner as before and stamp stems onto image panel. Repeat to stamp a leaf as shown. Remove masks. Stamp ladybug onto lower right corner of panel. Color all images using markers. Adhere to card front.

Stamp "have a happy day" onto kraft cardstock. Cut out words as shown. Attach to card front using foam dots.

Cut an 11-inch length of ribbon; wrap around left side of card front as shown, securing ends at upper left corner of card front. Adhere red button to card front covering ribbon ends. Tie a bow with remaining length of ribbon and adhere over button. ✳

Sources: Cardstock, stamp sets, ribbon and button from Gina K. Designs; Memento dye ink marker from Tsukineko LLC; markers from Imagination International Inc.; adhesive foam dots from Plaid Enterprises Inc.; paper adhesive from Tombow USA.

*tip

Add a pierced border and connect dots with a marker for instant faux stitching!

Daisies for Baby

Stamp multicolored images to create an interesting background and focal point. For variety, try mint green with yellow for a gender-neutral card.

Sources: Cardstock, A Year of Flowers stamp set and Basket Blessings stamp set, ribbon and buttons from Gina K. Designs; Memento dye ink markers from Tsukineko LLC; corner rounder from EK Success; Lacey Circles (#S4-293) and Standard Circles LG (#S4-114) die templates from Spellbinders™ Paper Arts; scoring board, rolling embossing tool and double-sided adhesive from Scor-Pal Products; adhesive foam dots from Plaid Enterprises Inc.

April

Here Comes the Sun

No matter the season, a sunny card complete with sponged clouds and cut-out flowers will brighten anyone's day!

Form a 4¼ x 5½-inch side-folded card from turquoise cardstock.

Cut a 3¾ x 5-inch piece from white cardstock. Sponge blue ink onto white panel, creating a sky background as shown (Photo 1).

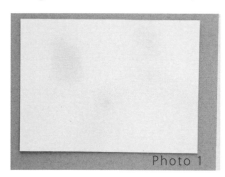

Photo 1

Adhere to brown cardstock; trim a small border.

Cut two 3¾ x 1¾-inch pieces from olive green cardstock. Referring to photo, cut a curved edge along top edge of both olive green panels; ink edges green (Photo 2).

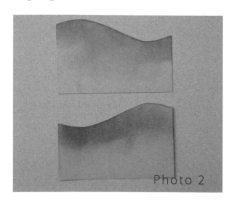

Photo 2

Layer and adhere olive green pieces to sky background as shown, using foam dots as desired to separate "hills."

Using brown ink, stamp a daisy onto printed paper. Cut out daisy, cutting slits between petals to create dimension (Photo 3).

Photo 3

Color center of daisy stamp with orange marker; stamp daisy center onto yellow cardstock. Punch out with ¾-inch circle punch (Photo 4).

Photo 4

Adhere daisy center to center of printed paper daisy with a foam dot.

In the same manner, apply orange ink to outer petals of the sunflower stamp. Stamp outer petals onto yellow cardstock (Photo 5).

Photo 5

Cut out flower and attach to layered panel as shown using foam dots and tucking flower behind olive green pieces.

Adhere one end of ¼-inch-wide ribbon to left side of layered panel ¾ inch below top edge of panel; wrap opposite end around bottom of panel and adhere to back, forming flower stem. Wrap ⅝-inch-wide ribbon around flower stem as shown; tie knot and trim ends.

Using foam dots, adhere daisy to layered panel as shown. Adhere panel to card front. ✱

Sources: Cardstock and stamp set from Gina K. Designs; printed paper from BasicGrey; distress ink pads from Ranger Industries Inc.; foam dots and paper adhesive from Tombow USA.

Materials

Cardstock: turquoise, white, dark brown,
 yellow, olive green
Curio Victoria printed paper
A Year of Flowers stamp set
Dye ink pads: brown, blue distress,
 green distress
Orange dye ink marker
Green grosgrain ribbon: 5½ inches
 ¼-inch-wide, 4½ inches ⅝-inch-wide
Sponge dauber
¾-inch circle punch
Adhesive foam dots
Paper adhesive

Easter Glory

Resembling a misty Easter-morning sunrise, layers of sponged colors make both a lovely background and focal point.

Project note: *Stamp all images with black ink. Create masks for all stamped images.*

Form a 4¼ x 5½-inch card from yellow cardstock.

Cut a 3⅞ x 5⅛-inch piece from white cardstock. Stamp three lilies onto white panel.

Stamp stems and leaves onto image panel as shown. Stamp one extra stem onto image panel below area where die-cut image panel will be placed.

Starting with lightest-color ink and using craft sponge, ink background of image panel pink, yellow and green being careful not to sponge color over stamped images. Color images using markers.

Adhere image panel to green cardstock; trim a small border. Adhere to card front.

Stamp a lily onto white cardstock. In the same manner as before, stamp a stem onto white cardstock. Cover with a mask. Using desired Long

Materials
Cardstock: yellow, white, green
Stamp sets: A Year of Flowers, Pressed Flowers
Dye ink pads: black, yellow, green distress, pink distress
Copic® markers: RV10, RV19, Y15, YG00, YG93, YG97
Long Classic Rectangles LG die templates (#S4-142)
Die-cutting and embossing machine
Craft sponge
Adhesive foam dots
Paper adhesive

Rectangles LG die template, die-cut and emboss a rectangle around masked images; do not remove die template (Photo 1).

With die template in place and starting with lightest color ink, sponge ink over die cut using pink, yellow and green (Photo 2).

Remove die template and masks. Color images using markers.

Stamp "Praise the Lord" onto die-cut rectangle. Adhere to green cardstock and trim a small border. Attach to card front as shown using foam dots, aligning stem on die-cut with stem on image panel. ✳

Photo 1

Photo 2

Sources: Cardstock and stamp sets from Gina K. Designs; Memento ink pads from Tsukineko LLC; markers from Imagination International Inc.; die templates from Spellbinders™ Paper Arts; adhesive foam dots from Plaid Enterprises Inc.; paper adhesive from Tombow USA.

Make a Wish

Soft purple sponging and a few cut petals create the look and feel of an evening sky and gentle spring breeze. Relax and enjoy!

Wishing you love joy & happiness

tip

I often use green like a neutral. Although I love brown and black for contrast, green always brings a fresh, nature feel to your card and goes with all of your flowers and colors.

Sources: Cardstock, A Year of Flowers stamp set and Many Wishes stamp set from Gina K. Designs; Memento ink pads from Tsukineko LLC; Copic® markers from Imagination International Inc.; small corner rounder from EK Success; Petite Ovals SM (#S4-140) and Petite Ovals LG (#S4-138) die templates from Spellbinders™ Paper Arts; adhesive foam dots from Plaid Enterprises Inc.; double-sided adhesive from Tombow USA.

May
Paper Roses

Paper tole is the art of layering several portions of the same image over and over to build dimension. Flower stamps are perfect for tole, and roses, with their many-layered petals, are especially magnificent with this technique!

Form a 5½ x 4¼-inch card from bright pink cardstock. Round right corners of card front.

Cut a 5¼ x 4-inch piece from white cardstock. Using 2¾-inch Standard Circles LG die template, emboss a circle onto white panel ⅝ inch from left edge of panel and ¾ inch above bottom edge. Round right corners of white panel.

Stamp sentiment onto lower right corner of panel as shown. Wrap ribbon horizontally around center of white panel; secure ends to back using paper adhesive. Adhere to card front.

Stamp rose four times onto a 3¾ x 5½-inch piece of bright pink cardstock; reink stamp between stamping (Photo 1).

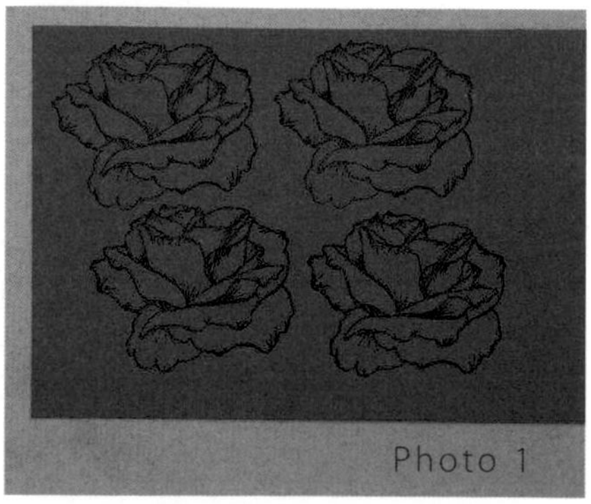

Cut out one whole rose and selected pieces from remaining roses (Photo 2).

Photo 2

Using foam dots, attach rose layers to rose (Photo 3). **Note:** *Trim foam dots as needed to fit on backs of small rose pieces.*

Stamp two leaves onto green cardstock. Cut out leaves and adhere them to back of layered rose. Adhere to card front as shown. ✳

Sources: Cardstock and stamp sets from Gina K. Designs; Memento dye ink pad from Tsukineko LLC; die templates from Spellbinders™ Paper Arts; paper adhesive from Tombow USA.

tip

Try this same layout turning the card so the ribbon runs vertically down the middle and the greeting is in lower right corner.

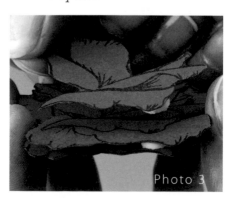

Photo 1

Photo 3

Materials

Cardstock: bright pink, white, green
Masking material
Stamp sets: A Year of Flowers,
    Say It With Flowers
Black dye ink pad
6 inches ⅝-inch-wide black/white
    stitched ribbon
Small corner rounder
Standard Circles LG die templates
    (#S4-114)
Die-cutting and embossing machine
Adhesive foam dots
Paper adhesive

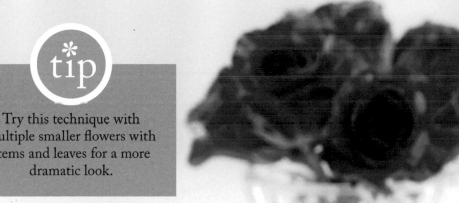

tip

Try this technique with multiple smaller flowers with stems and leaves for a more dramatic look.

have a
beautiful
Mother's
Day!

Crazy Daisies

Add more whimsy to these circular-shape flowers with the spotlighting technique and punches. Matching printed papers in contrasting colors will really make your spotlighting pop!

Materials
Cardstock: yellow, red, white, purple
Crazy Daisy Digital printed papers:
   green, purple, yellow
A Year of Flowers stamp set
Black dye ink pad
Circle punches: ¾-inch, ⅞-inch, 1-inch,
   1¼-inch, 1⅜-inch
Adhesive foam dots
Paper adhesive
Computer with color printer

Form a 4¼ x 5½-inch card from yellow cardstock.

Using computer with color printer, print three 3⅞ x 5⅛-inch pieces of Crazy Daisy paper: one green, one yellow and one purple. Adhere green printed paper panel to red cardstock; trim a small border. Adhere to card front.

Referring to photo throughout, punch the following circles: three 1¼-inch circles and one ¾-inch circle from purple printed paper, one 1-inch circle from yellow printed paper, three 1⅜-inch circles and one ⅞-inch circle from red cardstock, and one 1¼-inch circle from purple cardstock (Photo 1).

Photo 1

Layer and adhere circles to card front as shown, using foam dots to pop up layered circles as desired (Photo 2).

Photo 2

Stamp two flowers onto white cardstock. Cut out each flower, trimming between petals as desired. Layer and adhere flowers to lower right corner of card front as shown.

Stamp "FOR YOU" onto red cardstock. Punch a ¾-inch circle around sentiment. Attach to center of layered flower using a foam dot. ✳

Sources: Cardstock, Crazy Daisy Digital papers and stamp set from Gina K. Designs; Memento ink pad from Tsukineko LLC; circle punches and corner rounder from EK Success; adhesive foam dots from Plaid Enterprises Inc.; paper adhesive from Tombow USA.

tip

Make large layered daisies to keep on hand as the perfect fast finish to any card design.

Your Special Day

Including metallic papers and glitter for additional sparkle makes a bride's card extra special.

tip

With the tole technique, you can arrange the top layer of petals pointing outward to create a more fully bloomed tulip, adding more variety to your arrangement.

Sources: Cardstock, A Year of Flowers stamp set and Arranged With Love stamp set from Gina K. Designs; Memento ink pad from Tsukineko LLC; Copic® markers from Imagination International Inc.; self-adhesive pearls from Mark Richards Enterprises Inc.; Labels Four die templates (#S4-190) from Spellbinders™ Paper Arts; glitter glue from Ranger Industries Inc.; adhesive foam dots from Plaid Enterprises Inc.; double-sided adhesive from Tombow USA.

June

You're a Blessing Dad

Can you send flowers to a man? Yes, you can! Choose clean lines, muted, earthy colors, and faux-linen texture for a back-to-nature card that's sure to please.

you're such a blessing dad

Form a 4¼ x 5½-inch card from tan cardstock.

Cut a 3⅞ x 5⅛-inch piece from white glossy cardstock. Distress glossy side of cardstock by pulling sanding block from top to bottom as shown. This will create fine straight scratches on surface of panel. Rotate panel and repeat process creating straight scratches perpendicular to first scratches (Photo 1).

Photo 1

Using green ink, stamp leaves randomly onto edges of glossy panel, allow some leaves to extend past panel's edges. In the same manner, stamp flowers onto edges of panel with brown ink (Photo 2).

Photo 2

Note: *When stamping leaves and flowers, do not reink between stamping each image as this will produce different shades of leaves and flowers.*

Sponge green ink onto glossy panel, making some areas darker than others (Photo 3).

Photo 3

Using brown ink pad, ink directly onto panel as shown (Photo 4).

Photo 4

Adhere to dark brown cardstock; trim a small border. Wrap ribbon around layered panel as shown. Adhere right end of ribbon to back of panel and allow left end to extend past edge of panel. Use paper piercer to fray left end of ribbon as desired. Wrap jute around left end of ribbon; tie knot and trim ends. Adhere panel to card front.

Use brown ink to stamp leaves onto green cardstock; cut out. Tuck stem of leaves under jute knot and secure with paper adhesive.

Stamp sentiment onto tan cardstock with brown ink. Using

2⅜ x 1⅝-inch Petite Ovals LG die template, die-cut and emboss an oval around sentiment.

Using 2⅜ x 1⅞-inch Classic Rectangles LG die template, die-cut and emboss a rectangle from dark brown cardstock. Pierce holes through upper left and lower right corners of rectangle; insert brads.

Using foam dots, layer and attach die cuts to card front as shown. ✷

Sources: Cardstock and stamp sets from Gina K. Designs; distress ink pad and sanding block from Ranger Industries Inc.; die templates from Spellbinders™ Paper Arts; paper adhesive from Scor-Pal Products.

Materials

Cardstock: tan, dark brown, green, white glossy
Stamp sets: A Year of Flowers, Masculine Messages
Dye ink pads: brown, green distress
2 small brown matte brads
7 inches ⅝-inch-wide brown/white stitched ribbon
Natural jute
Die templates: Classic Rectangles LG (#S4-132), Petite Ovals LG (#S4-138)
Die-cutting and embossing machine
Sanding block
Paper piercer
Craft sponge
Adhesive foam dots
Paper adhesive

*tip

Try this same design using blues in place of the greens and browns for a denim look.

For You

Use earthy colors for a masculine card, or bright and pastel colors for the look of madras shorts. Add a hint of glitter for summer sparkle!

Form a 4¼ x 5½-inch card from black cardstock.

Cut a 4 x 5¼-inch piece from white cardstock. Drag edge of yellow ink pad vertically along white panel and then drag edge of ink pad along panel horizontally (Photo 1).

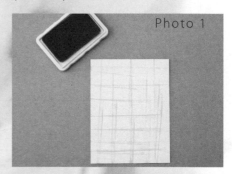

Photo 1

Repeat twice, first with aqua ink pad (Photo 2) and then with pink ink pad (Photo 3).

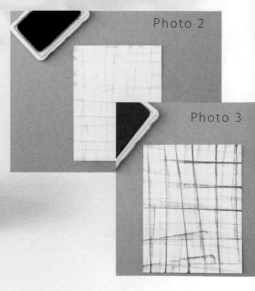

Photo 2

Photo 3

Stamp three flowers onto plaid panel with black ink, allowing images to extend past edges of panel. In the same manner, stamp "for you" onto lower right corner of panel. Adhere panel to card front.

Stamp a flower onto white cardstock with black ink; stamp a ladybug onto one of the flower petals. Using a 1¼-inch circle punch, punch three circles from flower, including the ladybug on one circle. Color circles using markers as shown. Apply glitter to circles as desired using glue pen. Let dry.

Punch three 1⅜-inch circles from black cardstock. Adhere flower circles to black circles. Adhere circles to card front as shown with foam dots, aligning flower circles with corresponding sections of flowers on card front. ✳

Sources: Cardstock and A Year of Flowers stamp set from Gina K. Designs; black Memento ink pad from Tsukineko LLC; Vivid ink pads from Clearsnap Inc.; circle punches from EK Success; adhesive foam dots from Plaid Enterprises Inc.; double-sided tape from Scor-Pal Products; glue pen from Sakura of America.

Materials
Cardstock: black, white
A Year of Flowers stamp set
Dye ink pads: black, yellow, pink, aqua
Copic® markers: B02, BG05, R83, RV19, Y15, Y17
Clear glitter
Circle punches: 1¼-inch, 1⅜-inch
Adhesive foam dots
Glue pen
Double-sided paper adhesive

Blessings

Create more than one colored panel of faux linen for your project; it adds more interest to the layout and looks like swatches of fabric on your card. Yellow and green look so fresh and summery with red, white and blue.

Sources: Cardstock, A Year of Flowers stamp set, Say It With Flowers stamp set, ribbon and buttons from Gina K. Designs; Memento ink pad from Tsukineko LLC; distress ink pads from Ranger Industries Inc.; Petite Ovals SM die templates (#S4-140) from Spellbinders™ Paper Arts; adhesive foam dots from Plaid Enterprises Inc.; double-sided adhesive from Tombow USA.

July
Celebrate

Just in time for summer birthdays, creatively stamped blooms take on the appearance of explosive fireworks. Embossed images on glossy cardstock are sponged with ink to create a look that allows your embossing to shine through.

Celebrate

Materials

Cardstock: red, white matte, light blue, dark blue, white glossy
Stamp sets: A Year of Flowers, Festive Frame
Ink pads: watermark, blue dye
Blue fine-tip marker
Embossing powders: clear fine, red glitter
5½ inches ⅝ inch wide red/white stitched ribbon
2 silver brads
Petite Ovals SM die templates (#S4-140)
Die-cutting and embossing machine
Craft sponge
Embossing heat tool
Paper piercer
Antistatic pad or dryer sheet
Paper towels
Paper adhesive

Form a 5½ x 4¼-inch card from red cardstock.

Cut a 4¾ x 3½-inch piece from white glossy cardstock. Using watermark ink, stamp three small hydrangea images onto glossy panel; rub with antistatic pad or dryer sheet. Sprinkle with clear embossing powder; tap off extra and heat-emboss. *Note: Stamp and emboss flowers one at a time to ensure ink will stay wet enough for embossing powder to stick.*

Sponge blue ink onto stamped panel, leaving some white space. Make some areas darker to create the appearance of the night sky and drifting smoke. Wipe ink off of embossed flowers using paper towels (Photo 1).

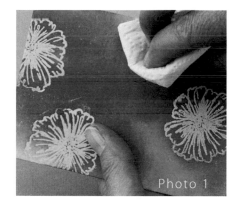

Photo 1

Using watermark ink, stamp daisy image onto center of panel. Sprinkle with red glitter embossing powder; tap off extra and heat-emboss (Photo 2).

Photo 2

Referring to photo, draw dotted lines leading from bottom edge of panel to bottom of flowers using fine-tip marker.

Adhere panel to dark blue cardstock; trim a small border.

Adhere to a 5⅛ x 3⅞-inch piece of light blue cardstock. Cut a V-notch at one end of ribbon; wrap ribbon around layered panel as shown, securing right end to back of panel. Secure left end of ribbon to front of panel, only applying adhesive to end of ribbon. Adhere panel to white cardstock; trim a small border. Adhere to card front.

Stamp "Celebrate" onto white matte cardstock with blue ink. Using 2 x ⅞-inch Petite Ovals SM die template, die-cut and emboss an oval around sentiment. Pierce holes on each side of sentiment; insert brads. Adhere to card front as shown. ✳

Sources: Cardstock and stamp sets from Gina K. Designs; VersaMark watermark ink pad from Tsukineko LLC; embossing powders from Ranger Industries Inc.; die templates from Spellbinders™ Paper Arts; paper adhesive from Scor-Pal Products.

✳tip

Try using multiple colors of glitter embossing powder to create a sparkly look.

Gilded Lilies

Embossed flowers in elegant silver or gold are the perfect elements for a card that will touch a couple's hearts on their wedding or anniversary. The traditional color scheme is black tie all the way!

Materials
Cardstock: black, white, gold
Stamp sets: A Year of Flowers,
    A Beautiful Life
Watermark ink pad
Gold super-fine embossing powder
3 gold brads
Die templates: Classic Rectangles LG
    (#S4-132), Classic Rectangles SM
    (#S4-130)
Die-cutting and embossing machine
Piercing tool
Embossing heat tool
Adhesive foam dots
Double-sided tape

Form a 5½ x 4¼-inch card from black cardstock.

Cut a 5¼ x 4-inch panel from white cardstock; set aside.

Stamp lilies, stems and leaves onto white cardstock. Sprinkle with embossing powder; heat-emboss. Using 2⅞ x 3¾-inch Classic Rectangles LG die template, die-cut and emboss a rectangle around embossed image (Photo 1).

Photo 1

Adhere to gold cardstock; trim a small border. Adhere to 5¼ x 4-inch white cardstock panel as shown.

In the same manner, stamp and emboss sentiment onto white cardstock. Using 1⅞ x 2⅜-inch Classic Rectangles SM die template, die-cut and emboss a rectangle around sentiment. In the same manner, die-cut and emboss a 2⅛ x 2¾-inch rectangle from gold cardstock. Attach sentiment die cut to gold die cut using foam dots. Adhere to black cardstock; trim a small border. Adhere to white panel as shown with foam dots.

Pierce three holes below sentiment die cut; insert brads. Adhere to card front. ✳

Sources: Cardstock and stamp sets from Gina K. Designs; VersaMark watermark ink pad from Tsukineko LLC; super-fine embossing powder from Ranger Industries Inc.; die templates from Spellbinders™ Paper Arts; adhesive foam dots from Plaid Enterprises Inc.; double-sided tape from Scor-Pal Products.

Welcome Little One

Clean lines and classic shapes, without fancy borders and frills, make this card perfect for welcoming a baby boy. Emboss the daisy with clear or white embossing powder; sponge blue ink on and wipe it off again to reveal the design.

Sources: Cardstock, A Year of Flowers stamp set, Basket Blessings stamp set, ribbon and button from Gina K. Designs; Memento ink pad and Memento dye ink marker from Tsukineko LLC; distress ink pad from Ranger Industries Inc.; small corner rounder from EK Success; Standard Circles LG die templates (#S4-114) from Spellbinders™ Paper Arts; rolling embossing tool, scoring board and double-sided tape from Scor-Pal Products; adhesive foam dots from Plaid Enterprises Inc.

August
Floral Fantasy

Reverse masking gives you the ability to add depth and layers to your card without adding bulk. The simple, classic look is a showstopper!

Materials
Cardstock: light blue, white, red, pink
Scrap paper
A Year of Flowers stamp set
Dye ink pads: red, green, aqua
Markers: green, pink
Buttons: 1 red, 1 lime green, 1 blue
Craft sponge or sponge dauber
Adhesive foam dots
Repositionable tape
Paper adhesive

Form a 4¼ x 5½-inch card from light blue cardstock.

Cut a 3¾ x 5-inch piece from white cardstock. Cut a 3¾ x 5-inch piece from scrap paper. Cut a 2⅞ x 3¾-inch rectangle from center of scrap paper panel, creating a frame to act as a mask. Attach frame mask to white cardstock panel using repositionable tape and aligning edges (Photo 1).

Photo 1

Stamp flowers onto white cardstock panel with red ink as shown. Stamp leaves with green ink (Photo 2).

Photo 2

Sponge aqua ink onto white panel, leaving white space as shown. Remove mask (Photo 3).

Photo 3

Color flowers and leaves using markers. Adhere panel to red cardstock; trim a small border. Adhere to card front.

Cut a thin strip from pink cardstock and two thin strips from red cardstock. Thread cardstock strips through buttons and knot on front or back as desired; trim ends. Attach buttons to card front as shown using foam dots. ✳

Source: Cardstock, stamp set and buttons from Gina K. Designs.

Beautiful Friend...

Use the reverse-masking technique to create a beautiful backdrop that pushes your main image to the foreground for a design that's both elegant and charming.

tip

Double-sided tape helps ribbons lay flat. Cutting your ribbon and adhering it to the back edges of your mats with the tape instead of using a longer length to wrap and tie all the way around saves ribbon and money!

Project note: Stamp all images and sentiment using black ink.

Form a 5½ x 4¼-inch card from black cardstock.

Cut a 5¼ x 4-inch piece from white cardstock. Stamp a rose onto white panel as shown. Color rose on white panel using markers.

Stamp stem and leaves onto white panel as shown. Color stem and leaves on white panel using markers.

Stamp sentiment onto image panel as shown.

Using 2¾-inch Standard Circles LG die template, die-cut

a circle from a 5¼ x 4-inch piece of scrap paper (Photo 1).

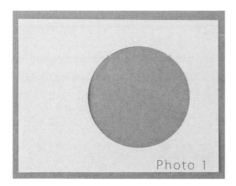

Photo 1

Position scrap paper piece over image panel as shown; secure with repositionable tape. Using craft sponge or sponge dauber, ink circle yellow (Photo 2). Remove mask.

Photo 2

Cut a 5½-inch length from ribbon. Wrap around left side of panel as shown; secure ends to back. Adhere to card front. Tie a double bow with remaining ribbon. Attach to card front as shown using an adhesive dot. ✻

Sources: Cardstock, stamp sets and ribbon from Gina K. Designs; Memento ink pads from Tsukineko LLC; Copic® markers from Imagination International Inc.; die templates from Spellbinders™ Paper Arts; double-sided tape from Scor-Pal Products.

Materials
Cardstock: black, white
Scrap paper
Stamp sets: A Year of Flowers, Arranged
    With Love
Dye ink pads: black, yellow
Copic® markers: G99, R29, R59, YG03
19½ inches ⅝-inch-wide black/white
    stitched ribbon
Standard Circles LG die templates (#S4-114)
Die-cutting machine
Craft sponge or sponge dauber
Adhesive dots
Repositionable tape
Double-sided tape

Congrats!

Sponge cool blue and soft green ink over a reverse-masked area to create a landscape that instantly takes your flowers outside.

Sources: Cardstock, A Year of Flowers stamp set, Arranged With Love stamp set and ribbon from Gina K. Designs; Memento ink pad and Memento dye ink markers from Tsukineko LLC; distress ink pads and gel pen from Ranger Industries Inc.; Classic Ovals SM die templates (#S4-112) from Spellbinders™ Paper Arts; double-sided tape, Scor-Buddy and Scor-Bug embossing tool from Scor-Pal Products.

September
For You

Here is a fun way to display your beautiful stamped designs—
an easel card! One fold transforms ordinary cards
into little works of art.

Project note: *Use black ink through-out unless otherwise directed.*

Form a 4¼ x 5½-inch card from dark brown cardstock. Adhere a 4 x 5¼-inch piece of white card-stock to card front (Photo 1).

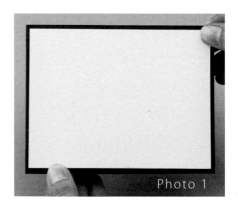

Photo 1

Open card and lay it on scoring board with long edge horizontal on work surface as shown. Score a vertical line 2¾ inches from left edge (Photo 2).

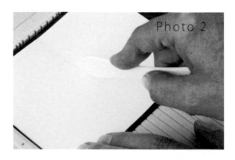

Photo 2

Mountain-fold at scored line to create an easel-style card base.

Stamp three sunflowers onto white cardstock; color with markers. In the same manner, stamp three sunflowers onto masking material and cut out. Cover colored sunflowers with masking sunflowers.

Stamp leaves around colored sunflowers, overlapping masked sunflowers as desired. Remove masks and color leaves with markers (Photo 3).

Photo 3

Cut out colored image as shown. Using watermark ink, stamp roses randomly onto ivory cardstock. Sprinkle with embossing powder;

heat-emboss. Sponge black ink over embossed roses. Remove excess ink from embossed roses using paper towels. Using 2⅞ x 4½-inch Labels Fourteen die template, die-cut a partial label around embossed roses to create a vase shape. Attach to bottom half of card front using foam dots as shown (Photo 4).

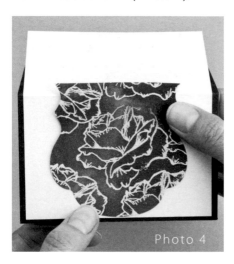

Photo 4

Attach only bottom edge of cut-out flowers to top of vase using foam dots. This allows top of flowers to pop up when card is folded easel style (Photo 5). Stamp "for you" onto kraft cardstock. Cut a tag shape around words; punch a ⅛-inch hole

Photo 5

Cut a 4 x 5¼-inch piece from white cardstock. Stamp sunflower 1½ inches above bottom edge of white panel; color with markers. Adhere button to center of sunflower, creating a stopper for easel card. Stamp sentiment below sunflower. Adhere inside card. ✳

Sources: Cardstock and stamp sets from Gina K. Designs; Memento dye ink pad and VersaMark watermark ink pad from Tsukineko LLC; embossing powder from Ranger Industries Inc.; markers from Imagination International Inc.; die templates from Spellbinders™ Paper Arts; scoring board and tool from Scor-Pal Products.

tip

Any shaped card works with the easel technique. Try a round card or shaped dies for more variety; measure carefully to score through the middle of the card front.

through right end of tag. Thread ribbon through hole and tie a knot; trim ends. Adhere to card front using adhesive dots.

Materials
Cardstock: dark brown, white, ivory, kraft
Masking material
Stamp sets: A Year of Flowers,
    Say It With Flowers
Ink pads: black dye, watermark
Clear embossing powder
Copic® markers: E31, E37, G99, Y15,
    Y38, YG23
Large brown button
3 inches ⅜-inch-wide black/white
    gingham ribbon
⅛-inch hole punch
Labels Fourteen die templates (#S4-290)
Die-cutting machine
Paper towels
Scoring board and scoring tool
Embossing heat tool
Craft sponge
Adhesive foam dots
Adhesive dots
Paper adhesive

for you

All the flowers of all the tomorrows are in the seeds of today.

Beautiful Day

The torn edge of a piece of paper provides the perfect mask—
the stamped results are beautiful on this easel card!

Materials
Cardstock: green, ivory, blue
Scrap paper
Stamp sets: A Year of Flowers, A
    Beautiful Life
Green distress ink pad
Dye ink markers: blue, green
Iridescent glitter
Large green button
10 inches ⅝-inch-wide light green/
    green stitched ribbon
Scoring board and scoring tool
Embossing rolling tool
Craft sponge
Adhesive foam dots
Repositionable tape
Double-sided tape
Glue pen

Cut a 5½ x 8½-inch piece from green cardstock. With long edge horizontal on work surface, score vertical lines 4¼ inches and 6⅜ inches from left edge. Fold at scored lines to form a 5½ x 4¼-inch easel card.

Cut two 5¼ x 4-inch pieces from ivory cardstock; set one piece aside. Create torn mask by tearing a 5¼ x 4-inch piece of scrap paper in half, pulling paper back and forth while tearing to create textured edges. Referring to photo, place torn piece onto ivory panel and sponge green ink along torn edge. Reposition on other half of ivory panel and repeat inking process as shown (Photo 1).

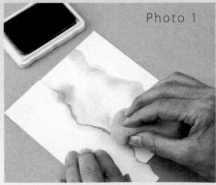

Photo 1

In the same manner, stamp flowers and leaves over inked area as shown, allowing some images to extend past masked area. Remove mask (Photo 2).

Photo 2

Stamp sentiment along right bottom edge of ivory panel. Emboss a dotted border along top and bottom edges using embossing rolling tool. Adhere to card front, only applying adhesive to bottom half of card front.

Stamp flowers onto ivory cardstock; color using markers. Apply glitter to flowers using glue pen. Cut out flowers, and layer and attach to card front as shown with foam dots.

Color desired sections of sentiment stamp with blue and green markers. Huff on stamp to reactivate ink and stamp onto remaining ivory panel as shown. Stamp a flower onto lower right corner of panel; color using markers. Apply glitter to flower using glue pen.

In the same manner as before, use embossing rolling tool to create a dotted border along bottom of panel.

Wrap ribbon around panel, forming a loop on right end as shown. Secure with double-sided tape, wrapping ends to back.

Cut a thin strip from blue cardstock. Thread strip through button and attach button to ribbon loop. Adhere panel inside card as shown. ✳

Sources: Cardstock, stamp sets, ribbon and button from Gina K. Designs; distress ink pad from Ranger Industries Inc.; Memento dye ink markers from Tsukineko LLC; scoring board and tool, embossing rolling tool and double-sided tape from Scor-Pal Products; adhesive foam dots from Plaid Enterprises Inc.; glue pen from Sakura of America.

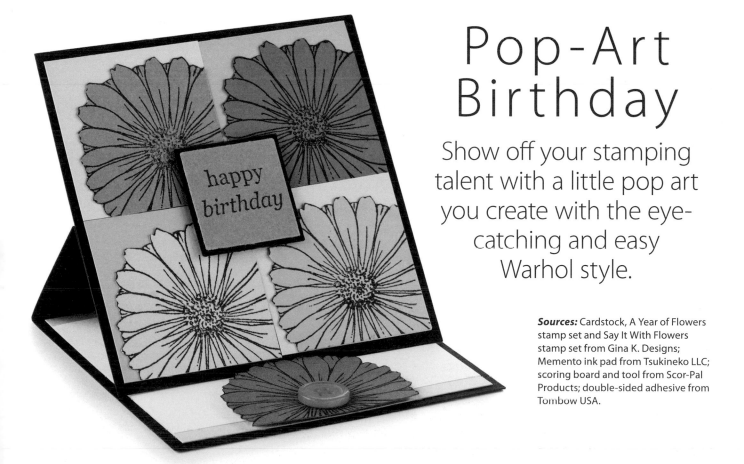

Pop-Art Birthday

Show off your stamping talent with a little pop art you create with the eye-catching and easy Warhol style.

Sources: Cardstock, A Year of Flowers stamp set and Say It With Flowers stamp set from Gina K. Designs; Memento ink pad from Tsukineko LLC; scoring board and tool from Scor-Pal Products; double-sided adhesive from Tombow USA.

October
Irresistible Daisies

A crayon box contains a key tool for a resist stamping technique—the beautiful results will amaze you!

Form a 5½ x 4¼-inch card from yellow cardstock. Referring to photo, adhere a 5⅛ x 3⅞-inch piece of orange cardstock to card front at an angle.

Cut a 5¼ x 3¾-inch piece from white glossy cardstock. Stamp three overlapping flowers onto glossy panel with black ink. Add stamped leaves as desired (Photo 1).

tip

For solid white petals, fill in the entire area of each petal with crayon. Make the coloring sketchy for a more whimsical look.

Sponge yellow, green and orange inks onto glossy panel, using circular motions to blend colors together (Photo 3).

Photo 1

Use white crayon to scribble a loop inside each flower petal (Photo 2).

Photo 2

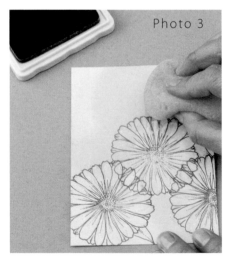

Photo 3

Gently rub off crayon scribbles with a paper towel to reveal white space (Photo 4).

Photo 4

Color flowers and leaves using markers. Referring to photo, draw a border around image panel using gel pen. Adhere to card front as shown.

Wrap ribbon around top of card front; tie a knot on right side and trim ends.

Cut a thin strip from yellow cardstock. Thread strip through button; tie knot on top, trim ends. Adhere button to ribbon knot. *

Sources: Cardstock, stamp set and button from Gina K. Designs; Memento dye ink markers from Tsukineko LLC; distress ink pad from Ranger Industries Inc.; gel pen from Sakura of America.

Materials

Cardstock: white matte, white glossy, orange, yellow
Masking material (optional)
A Year of Flowers stamp set
Dye ink pads: black, yellow, orange, green distress
Dye ink markers: orange, green
Black gel pen
White crayon
15 inches ⅝-inch-wide brown/white stitched ribbon
Large yellow button
Craft sponge or sponge dauber
Paper towel
Double-sided adhesive

Sunset Spectrum

Use a brayer to roll ink over a crayon-resist design on glossy cardstock. Cutting your scene into pieces makes each part a mini art canvas.

Project note: *Create and use masks if desired for stamped images.*

Form a 5½ x 4¼-inch card from dark brown cardstock. Adhere a 5¼ x 4-inch piece of white cardstock to card front.

Cut a 4¾ x 3¾-inch piece from white glossy cardstock. Using dark brown ink, stamp flowers onto glossy panel as shown; let dry completely (Photo 1).

Photo 1

Color over stamped images using crayon (Photo 2).

Photo 2

Materials
Cardstock: dark brown, white, white glossy
A Year of Flowers stamp set
Dye ink pads: dark brown, multicolored autumn colors
Copic® markers: various greens
White crayon
Rubber brayer
Paper towels
Adhesive foam dots
Double-sided tape

Use rubber brayer to apply multicolored inks onto image panel; let dry completely (Photo 3).

white areas. If desired, color leaves and stems using green markers (Photo 4).

Photo 5

Photo 3

Photo 4

Gently rub crayon off of glossy panel with a paper towel to reveal

Cut image panel into three pieces (Photo 5). Adhere to card front as shown. ✳

Sources: Cardstock and A Year of Flowers stamp set from Gina K. Designs; Memento dye ink pad and Kaleidacolor ink pad from Tsukineko LLC; markers from Imagination International Inc.; adhesive foam dots from Plaid Enterprises Inc.; double-sided tape from Scor-Pal Products.

Moonlit Flowers

An unlikely combination of colors makes up this eye-catching resist and masked Halloween design!

Sources: Cardstock, A Year of Flowers stamp set, and Buds and Vase stamp set from Gina K. Designs; Memento dye ink pads from Tsukineko LLC; Vivid ink pad from Clearsnap Inc.; button from BasicGrey; corner rounder from EK Success; Standard Circles LG die templates (#S4-114) from Spellbinders™ Paper Arts; double-sided adhesive from Tombow USA.

November

Grateful

An inexpensive household item like bleach takes your cards to another level, producing new and often unexpected colors in your cardstock, like changing leaves that are just right for your fall projects.

Materials

Cardstock: orange, burnt orange, black, dark brown, kraft
Fall-color printed paper
Stamp sets: A Year of Flowers, Say It With Flowers
Ink pads: watermark, black dye, light brown distress
Copic® marker: YG23
Super-fine embossing powder: black, clear
Bleach
15 inches ⅝-inch-wide black/white gingham ribbon
Circle punches: 1¼-inch, 1⅜-inch
Classic Scalloped Circles LG die templates (#S4-124)
Die-cutting and embossing machine
Embossing heat tool
Sponge dauber
Paper towels
Glass dish
Cotton swab
Adhesive foam dots
Double-sided tape

Project note: Do not use a glass dish that is used for cooking.

Form 5½ x 4¼-inch card from orange cardstock.

Cut a 5 x 3¾-inch piece from burnt orange cardstock. Fold a paper towel multiple times and place inside glass dish; pour enough bleach over paper towel to saturate it. This creates a bleach ink pad.

Press sunflower stamp onto bleach ink pad and stamp sunflower onto burnt orange panel. Repeat, reinking stamp each time, letting some sunflowers extend past edges (Photo 1).

Photo 1

Note: Always clean stamps after using bleach on them. Let dry completely. In the same manner, stamp leaves onto panel. Adhere to black cardstock; trim a small border.

Using desired size Classic Scalloped Circles LG die template, die-cut and emboss a scalloped circle from printed paper. Attach to center top of burnt orange panel using foam dots.

Stamp two sunflowers onto orange cardstock and one sunflower onto dark brown cardstock with watermark ink. Sprinkle one orange sunflower and dark brown

sunflower with clear embossing powder; heat-emboss. Sprinkle remaining orange sunflower with black embossing powder; heat-emboss. Use a cotton swab to apply bleach to embossed sunflowers as desired; let dry completely. Reapply color to bleached sunflowers using marker and light brown distress ink as desired. Cut out sunflowers and attach to burnt orange panel as shown using foam dots.

Stamp "grateful" onto kraft cardstock. Punch a 1¼-inch circle around word. Punch a 1⅜-inch circle from

*tip

Different cardstock colors react differently to bleach: Some colors turn completely white, some fade to a paler shade of the original color, and a few, although not often, don't bleach at all! Test bleach on the different colors of cardstock you have and keep a sample for future reference.

black cardstock. Adhere circles together and adhere to burnt orange panel as shown with a foam dot.

Wrap ribbon around burnt orange panel, tie knot and trim ends as shown. Adhere to card front. ✳

Sources: Cardstock and stamp sets from Gina K. Designs; VersaMark watermark ink pad and Memento dye ink pad from Tsukineko LLC; distress ink pad and clear embossing powders from Ranger Industries Inc.; Copic® marker from Imagination International Inc.; die templates from Spellbinders™ Paper Arts; adhesive foam dots from Plaid Enterprises Inc.; double-sided adhesive from Scor-Pal Products.

tip

Try putting some bleach in a misting bottle to spray onto cardstocks for a gorgeous bleached splatter effect.

grateful

Sunflowers in Autumn

The bleaching technique allows you to remove color from darker cardstocks as if by magic. This is a lovely way to make multicolored patterned papers with stamps and darker-color cardstocks.

Materials

Cardstock: yellow, red, green
Masking material (optional)
A Year of Flowers stamp set
Ink pads: watermark, brown dye, green distress
Bleach
Clear embossing powder
Red button
Natural jute
Sponge dauber or craft sponge
Paintbrush
Distressing tool
Embossing heat tool
Adhesive foam dots

Project note: *Emboss image first to resist bleach and keep your image crisp.*

Form a 5½ x 4¼-inch card from yellow cardstock.

Cut a 5¼ x 4-inch piece from red cardstock; distress edges using distressing tool as desired.

Cut a 5 x 3¾-inch piece from green cardstock. Stamp sunflowers and leaves onto green panel with watermark ink. Sprinkle with embossing powder; heat-emboss.

In the same manner, stamp one sunflower onto red cardstock and emboss.

Pour a little bit of bleach into lid of container. Dip paintbrush into bleach and paint flowers on green cardstock and red cardstock (Photo 1).

Sponge brown ink onto centers of flowers on green panel (Photo 2). Cut out red flower. Cut green panel into three 1¾ x 3¾-inch pieces and distress edges (Photo 3).

Photo 3

Photo 2

Photo 1

Sponge brown ink on edges of green strips.

Attach green panels and red

flower to distressed red panel as shown. Wrap jute around panel as shown; secure ends to back. Adhere to card front.

Cut two small lengths of jute. Wrap jute around twine on card front as shown; thread jute through button. Tie knot on front; trim long tails. Attach button to card front as shown. ✳

Sources: Cardstock, stamp set and button from Gina K. Designs; distress ink pad from Ranger Industries Inc.; gel pen from Sakura of America.

Bleached Roses

Try this color combo for a sophisticated Veterans Day card. This design would also be lovely to recognize a grandparent on Grandparents Day.

Sources: Cardstock, A Year of Flowers stamp set and Arranged With Love stamp set from Gina K. Designs; Memento dye ink pads from TsukIneko LLC; Fancy Tags One die templates (#S4-235) from Spellbinders™ Paper Arts; adhesive foam dots from Plaid Enterprises Inc.; double-sided adhesive from Scor-Pal Products.

December

Frosted Poinsettias

White embossing on vellum is a stunning combination for elegant cold-weather cards. Coloring the back of vellum makes white accents pop and gives flowers a frosted appearance.

Form a 5½ x 4¼-inch card from dark blue cardstock.

Cut a 5¼ x 4-inch piece from light blue cardstock. Stamp poinsettias randomly onto light blue panel with watermark ink, allowing some flowers to extend past edge of panel (Photo 1).

Photo 1

Adhere to card front.

Cut a 4¾ x 3½-inch piece from vellum; rub vellum with antistatic or dryer sheet. In the same manner as before, stamp poinsettias onto vellum panel; sprinkle with embossing powder and heat-emboss (Photo 2).

Photo 2

Flip vellum panel over; color poinsettias using markers (Photo 3).

Photo 3

Flip vellum panel over to front and sponge blue ink on edges.

Using scoring board and scoring tool, score a border ⅛ inch from edges on vellum panel. *Note: Do not score over stamped images.*

Referring to photo, embellish panel with nailheads and rhinestones. Adhere panel to card front, placing adhesive where it will be hidden by nailheads and rhinestones.

Stamp "Season's Greetings!" onto light blue cardstock with dark blue ink. Using 2⅛ x 1⅝-inch Classic Rectangles SM die template, die-cut and emboss a rectangle around sentiment. With die template still in place, sponge blue ink onto die cut. Remove die template.

Adhere sentiment to dark blue cardstock; trim a small border. Attach to card front using foam dots. ✳

Sources: Cardstock and stamp sets from Gina K. Designs; Memento dye ink pad and VersaMark watermark ink pad from Tsukineko LLC; distress ink pad and embossing powder from Ranger Industries Inc.; markers from Imagination International Inc.; nailheads and self-adhesive rhinestones from Mark Richards Enterprises Inc.; die templates from Spellbinders™ Paper Arts; scoring board and scoring tool from Scor-Pal Products; adhesive dots and paper adhesive from Tombow USA.

Materials

Cardstock: dark blue, light blue
Vellum
Masking material
Stamp sets: A Year of Flowers, Festive Frame
Ink pads: dark blue, blue distress, watermark
White embossing powder
Copic® markers: B29, B97, G99, YG63
2mm silver nailheads
2 (5mm) silver self-adhesive rhinestones
Classic Rectangles SM die templates (#S4-130)
Die-cutting machine
Antistatic pad or dryer sheet
Paper towels
Scoring board and scoring tool
Embossing heat tool
Craft sponge
Adhesive foam dots
Paper adhesive

*tip

To adhere the vellum panel to card front, place strips of adhesive behind stamped images or embellishments to keep the adhesive from showing through the translucent panel.

Stained Glass Elegance

Nothing conveys simple elegance as beautifully as vellum, and the colored pane allows for gorgeous frosted effects.

Materials
Cardstock: green, red, gold, white
Vellum
A Year of Flowers stamp set
Ink pads: watermark, tan distress, brown distress
Gold super-fine embossing powder
Copic® markers: G94, G99, R59
Petite Ovals LG die templates (#S4-138)
Die-cutting machine
Antistatic pad or dryer sheet (optional)
Embossing heat tool
Sponge dauber
Adhesive foam dots
Double-sided tape

Form a 4¼ x 5½-inch card from green cardstock.

Cut a 3½ x 4⅞-inch piece from white cardstock. Using watermark ink, stamp poinsettias randomly onto white panel. Sprinkle with embossing powder; heat-emboss.

Sponge tan ink onto image panel, leaving some white spaces. Repeat with brown ink (Photo 1).

Adhere panel to gold cardstock; trim a small border. Adhere to red cardstock; trim a border. Adhere layered panel to card front.

Using 4⅛ x 3-inch Petite Ovals LG die template, die-cut an oval from vellum. Stamp a poinsettia onto vellum oval with watermark ink. Sprinkle with embossing powder; heat-emboss. Color using markers (Photo 2). Adhere to card front.

Using 4⅛ x 3-inch and 3⅝ x 2½-inch Petite Ovals LG die templates, die-cut a frame from gold cardstock (Photo 3). Adhere over image oval. ✳

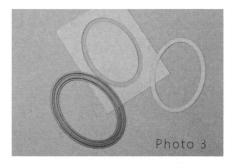

Photo 3

Photo 1

Photo 2

Sources: Cardstock and stamp set from Gina K. Designs; VersaMark watermark ink pad from Tsukineko LLC; distress ink pads and super-fine embossing powder from Ranger Industries Inc.; Copic® markers from Imagination International Inc.; die templates from Spellbinders™ Paper Arts; adhesive foam dots from Plaid Enterprises Inc.; double-sided adhesive from Scor-Pal Products.

Celebrate the Beauty

Extra layers of vellum petals over colored images add a delicate touch to your card designs. Using nontraditional colors creates an unexpected delight.

Sources: Cardstock, A Year of Flowers stamp set and Festive Frame stamp set from Gina K. Designs; Memento dye ink pads from Tsukineko LLC; Copic® markers from Imagination International Inc.; self-adhesive gems from Mark Richards Enterprises Inc.; Fancy Photo Corner punch from EK Success; Petite Ovals LG die templates (#S4-138) from Spellbinders™ Paper Arts; adhesive foam dots from Plaid Enterprises Inc.; double-sided adhesive from Scor-Pal Products.

Dates to Remember

January   **Cards needed** _____

_____   _____
_____   _____
_____   _____
_____   _____
_____   _____
_____   _____

February   **Cards needed** _____

_____   _____
_____   _____
_____   _____
_____   _____
_____   _____
_____   _____

March   **Cards needed** _____

_____   _____
_____   _____
_____   _____
_____   _____
_____   _____
_____   _____

April

Cards needed _____

_____ _____
_____ _____
_____ _____
_____ _____
_____ _____
_____ _____
_____ _____

May

Cards needed _____

_____ _____
_____ _____
_____ _____
_____ _____
_____ _____
_____ _____
_____ _____
_____ _____

June

Cards needed _____

_____ _____
_____ _____
_____ _____
_____ _____
_____ _____
_____ _____
_____ _____

Dates to Remember

July

Cards needed _____

_____

_____

_____

_____

_____

_____

_____

_____

_____

_____

_____

_____

August

Cards needed _____

_____

_____

_____

_____

_____

_____

_____

_____

_____

_____

_____

_____

September

Cards needed _____

_____

_____

_____

_____

_____

_____

_____

_____

_____

_____

_____

October

Cards needed _____

_____   _____
_____   _____
_____   _____
_____   _____
_____   _____
_____   _____
_____   _____

November

Cards needed _____

_____   _____
_____   _____
_____   _____
_____   _____
_____   _____
_____   _____
_____   _____

December

Cards needed _____

_____   _____
_____   _____
_____   _____
_____   _____
_____   _____
_____   _____
_____   _____

Buyer's Guide

BasicGrey
(801) 544-1116
www.basicgrey.com

Clearsnap Inc.
(800) 448-4862
www.clearsnap.com

EK Success
www.eksuccess.com

Gina K. Designs
(608) 838-3258
www.ginakdesigns.com

Imagination International Inc.
(541) 684-0013
www.copicmarker.com

Mark Richards Enterprises Inc.
(888) 901-0091
www.markrichardsusa.com

Plaid Enterprises Inc.
(800) 842-4197
www.plaidonline.com

Ranger Industries Inc.
(732) 389-3535
www.rangerink.com

Sakura of America
www.sakuraofamerica.com

Scor-Pal Products
(877) 629-9908
www.scor-pal.com

Spellbinders™ Paper Arts
(888) 547-0400
www.spellbinderspaper
arts.com

Tombow USA
www.tombowusa.com

Tsukineko LLC
(425) 883-7733
www.tsukineko.com

The Buyer's Guide listings are provided as a service to our readers and should not be considered an endorsement from this publication.

A Year of Flowers

EDITOR Tanya Fox

CREATIVE DIRECTOR Brad Snow

PUBLISHING SERVICES DIRECTOR Brenda Gallmeyer

MANAGING EDITOR Brooke Smith

GRAPHIC DESIGNER Nick Pierce

COPY SUPERVISOR Deborah Morgan

COPY EDITORS Rebecca Detwiler, Mary O'Donnell

TECHNICAL EDITOR Corene Painter

PHOTOGRAPHY SUPERVISOR Tammy Christian

PHOTO STYLISTS Tammy Liechty, Tammy Steiner

PHOTOGRAPHY Matthew Owen, Shane Pequignot

PRODUCTION ARTIST SUPERVISOR Erin Brandt

PRODUCTION ARTIST Amy Lin

PRODUCTION ASSISTANTS Marj Morgan, Judy Neuenschwander

ISBN: 978-1-59635-389-3
Printed in USA

1 2 3 4 5 6 7 8 9

A Year of Flowers is published by DRG, 306 East Parr Road, Berne, IN 46711. Printed in USA. Copyright © 2012 DRG. All rights reserved. This publication may not be reproduced in part or in whole without written permission from the publisher.

RETAIL STORES: If you would like to carry this pattern book or any other DRG publications, visit DRGwholesale.com.
Every effort has been made to ensure that the instructions in this publication are complete and accurate. We cannot, however, take responsibility for human error, typographical mistakes or variations in individual work. Please visit AnniesCustomerCare.com to check for pattern updates.